Seventy-Five Days of Prayers

Praying Through Pain,

Healing Through Faith

Written by Dr. LaQuita Parks

Pa-Pro-Vi
PUBLISHING

Cover Design:
Pa-Pro-Vi Publishing Creative Design Team

Printed in the United States of America.
ISBN: 978-1-959667-87-2
Library of Congress Control Number: 2025926477

For permission requests, please contact:
Pa-Pro-Vi Publishing
Email: support@paprovipublishing.com
Website: www.paprovipublishing.com

Contents

Dedication

This book is dedicated to every person who ever whispered a prayer on my behalf when I could not find the words for myself. To those who stood in the gap during my moments of chronic pain, illness, surgeries, and long nights at the Mayo Clinic. To those who prayed me through heartbreak, grief, loss, confusion, and motherhood's hardest seasons. Your prayers strengthened me more than you will ever know.

I also dedicate this book to every reader who is walking through their own storm. You are not alone. May you be reminded that prayer still works, prayer still heals, and prayer still reaches the heart of God.

With love and gratitude,
Dr. LaQuita Parks

Author's Note

Writing *Praying Through Pain, Healing Through Faith, 75 Days of Prayers* has been one of the most intimate and healing experiences of my life. Each prayer was born out of real moments, real struggles, real victories, and real encounters with the presence of God. I have lived through seasons when prayer was the only thing holding me together. And I have lived through seasons when my spirit was too tired to pray, but God surrounded me with people who prayed for me until I could stand again.

Prayer has carried me through chronic illnesses, physical limitations, emotional battles, brokenness, and the long medical journey that led me to the Mayo Clinic. Prayer has sustained me through the loss of loved *ones, the challenges of raising children, and the many unexpected chapters of my life story. Every time I felt like giving up, somebody prayed for me.*

My hope is that as you read these prayers, you feel strengthened, comforted, and reassured that God hears you. Whether your prayers are whispered, shouted, or held quietly in your heart, they matter. You matter.

Thank you for allowing me to walk beside you for 75 days.
And if you ever find yourself wondering whether anyone cares or whether anyone is praying for you, hear my heart clearly.

I am.

With love,
Dr. LaQuita Parks

Introduction

Prayer has always been my lifeline. It is the place where my heart finds rest, where my tears find meaning, and where my weary soul finds strength to keep going. I have lived enough life to know that prayer is not just a religious ritual. Prayer is connection. Prayer is comfort. Prayer is survival. And most of all, prayer is power.

The Bible tells us to "pray without ceasing," and for many years, I did not fully understand what that meant. But life has a way of teaching us lessons the heart cannot forget. I have walked through seasons when I felt so low, so broken, and so overwhelmed that I did not even know how to pray for myself. There were days I could only whisper, "Lord, help me." There were moments when the pain in my body and the weight in my spirit made prayer feel impossible.

Yet every single time, God sent someone to pray for me.

When chronic pain became my constant companion and my health battles grew heavier, somebody prayed for me. When I found myself at the Mayo Clinic, unsure of what answers would come next, somebody prayed for me. When illness tried to break my spirit, prayers held me together.

When I experienced deep loss and grief, and loved ones left this earth far sooner than my heart was ready to accept, somebody prayed for me.

When my children went through their own struggles and life took them down roads I wished they would never walk, somebody prayed for me.

When life felt overwhelming and I questioned my purpose, somebody prayed for me.

Those prayers carried me. Those prayers lifted me. Those prayers reminded me that God is always near, even in the darkest and most uncertain moments.

This book, 75 Days of Prayers, comes from that truth. It is written to give you comfort and assurance that prayer truly changes things. Sometimes the situation changes. Sometimes the answer comes. Sometimes the strength to endure grows. And often, we change.

Each prayer in these pages comes from my heart, shaped by my journey, my pain, my progress, my victories, and my unwavering belief that God hears us. No matter what you are facing, whether pain, confusion, fear, loss, hope, healing, or transition, this devotional is written to walk with you day by day, step by step, prayer by prayer.

So I ask you the same question God placed on my spirit:

Can we pray together?

Because I believe that when we pray together, we heal together.
And when we heal together, we become stronger than we ever imagined.

Let these 75 days remind you that you are seen, loved, and covered.
God is listening. God is moving. God is working. And God is with you always.

Day 1
But God

Thank you God for being our refuge and our strength. Friends, are you stuck at a point of pain? Are you struggling to rise from the ashes of your past? Are you so stagnant that you cannot see past your hurts? Is your physical pain causing you to question your spiritual truths? I could go on and on with the questions, but the answer will always remain the same. But God. He is the answer to our struggles, not the reason for them.

It is easy for some people to praise God in happy times and blame Him in difficult times. Oftentimes our past situations will cause us to question the light that is shining brightly before us because we do not trust the beauty. But God, in His power and His wisdom, has already worked it out on our behalf and for *our benefit. We must trust and believe that He is, He can, and He will see us through whatever we may be facing.*

I do not know about you friends, but my road has been paved with shards of glass that have done severe damage to my life. Yet instead of focusing on the destruction, I have made the choice to focus on the One who can repair my broken pieces. But God.

Continued prayers for me as I pray for you. Be blessed in your day. Loving you out loud, on purpose, with purpose.

Scripture:
"God is our refuge and strength, a very present help in trouble."
Psalm 46:1 (KJV)

Day 2
Let the Change Begin With Me

Thank you Lord God for the beauty of this day and for all the blessings it holds. Thank you for giving me yet another opportunity to encourage rather than discourage, to speak the positive instead of the negative, and to spread love and not hate. Help me to be a person who builds up and not one who tears down. Give me the strength to walk in a heavenly purpose so that I can truly be a blessing to those I come in contact with.

Let the change that I want to see in others start with me. Touch the hearts of each individual who reads this message and meet their needs in a tremendous way. Thank you for the forgiveness of sins and for sustaining us through your grace and mercy. In the

matchless name of Jesus the Son, I pray,
Amen.

Have an awesome day!

Scripture:
"Create in me a clean heart, O God, and renew
a right spirit within me."
Psalm 51:10 (KJV)

Day 3
In Spite of Myself

———— ❧ ————

Not because I have been so faithful, not because I have always obeyed, but because I have always trusted you to be with me every step of the way. Thank you Father God for your never failing love for me in spite of myself. Thank you for keeping me in the midst of it all in spite of myself. Be with me through this day and help me to remember that I should take no worry of tomorrow because all I have is right now.

Help me to shine in someone's life today. Forgive me for my sins and forgive those who do not understand the magnitude of your love. In the mighty name of Jesus I pray, Amen.

Scripture:

"Trust in the Lord with all your heart and lean not unto your own understanding. In all your ways acknowledge him and he shall direct your paths."

Proverbs 3:5–6 (KJV)

Day 4
Can I Pray for You?

―――――― ❦ ――――――

Heavenly Father, thank you for this day and all the beauty that it holds. Thank you for peace in the midst of a world filled with turmoil. Help us to find the joy in the middle of our pain and the sunshine after the rain. Keep the individuals reading this message safe and healthy. Meet their needs and calm their fears. We trust You and put our faith in You. Our hope is built on You. In the name of Jesus we pray, Amen.

Take time to be a blessing to someone today.

Scripture:
"You will keep him in perfect peace whose mind is stayed on you because he trusts in you."
Isaiah 26:3 (KJV)

Day 5
You Alone Are Our Hope

Thank you Father God for this day and all the beauty that it holds. We are grateful for every blessing you have bestowed upon us. As we seek to worship you today in spirit and in truth, help us to keep our minds and hearts focused on you. Bless us as we go through this day and help us to be a blessing to those we come into contact with.

Be with those who are sick, suffering, and grieving the loss of loved ones. Help us to stay grounded and at peace in the midst of our turmoil. Our faith and our trust are in You. You alone are our hope. Thank you for your love. In Jesus name we pray, Amen.

Scripture:

"The Lord is my strength and my shield. My heart trusted in him, and I am helped."
Psalm 28:7 (KJV)

Day 6
Today, Let Us Be the Answer

———— ❧ ————

Heavenly Father, thank You for waking us up this morning and giving us yet another opportunity to be a blessing to those we come in contact with. Whether in our personal lives or our professional lives, let us conduct ourselves as shining lights that are centered in love. Help us to be the calm in this world of chaos and the light at the end of someone's tunnel. Today is all we have, for tomorrow will take care of itself.

Today, let us be the answer to someone's prayers. The world would have us crippled in fear, but with You we are strong and filled with courage. Because of our faith in You, we are at peace. Forgive us when we do not trust You enough or when our faith grows weak. Walk with us on this journey day by day and help us increase in You as we decrease in ourselves. Thank You for Your grace and Your abundance of love. In Jesus name, Amen.

Scripture:
"Be strong and of good courage. Do not be afraid or dismayed, for the Lord your God is with you wherever you go."
Joshua 1:9 (KJV)

Day 7
Humble Hearts, Willing Hands

Father God, thank You for this day and for the beauty of the sun that shines so brightly in our lives. As we go through this day, remind us that when we humble ourselves before You, we widen the opportunity for You to do good in our lives and in the lives of others. Give us the strength and boldness to do Your work by doing good to others. Help us to honor You in all we do and say. Help us to use our gifts to be a blessing to those we come in contact with today. In Christ's name we pray, Amen.

Scripture:
"Humble yourselves in the sight of the Lord, and he shall lift you up."
James 4:10 (KJV)

Day 8
Peace Beyond Understanding

Father God, thank You so much for this day and for all the beauty it holds. Thank You for allowing us to wake up from a good night of sleep. Father, thank You for Your peace that passes all understanding. We know there is so much happening in the world today that is beyond our control, but we put our faith in You, we put our trust in You, and we put our hope in You. As we move through this day, help us to be a blessing to those we come in contact with. Help us to be the answer to somebody's prayers.

Father God, we ask that You bless us financially, bless us physically, and most importantly, bless us spiritually. We love You Father God because You first loved us. In the name of Jesus we pray, Amen.

Scripture:

"And the peace of God, which passes all understanding, shall keep your hearts and minds through Christ Jesus."

Philippians 4:7 (KJV)

Day 9
Mindful of Who You Are

Thank You Father for this day and for all the magnificent blessings You have so generously given us. Thank You for surrounding us with new opportunities to use the gifts You have given us so that we can be the answer to someone's prayers. Help us to strive to do what is right by You, by others, and by ourselves. Help us to be strong and steady as we position our lives in love and obedience toward You.

Help us to find peace in the midst of the chaos going on in our world. Help us to be mindful of those who need a little something extra today. As we go about our day, let us remain mindful of who You are, who we are, and who we aim to be. Forgive us when we overlook You and depend on the superficial. We thank You for

Your grace and Your mercy. In Christ we pray, Amen.

Scripture:
"Trust in the Lord, and do good. So shalt thou dwell in the land, and verily thou shalt be fed."
Psalm 37:3 (KJV)

Day 10
How Can I Help You?

Thank You Father God for this brand new day and for all the joy and beauty that it holds. There are so many among us who are sick, suffering, or mourning the loss of precious loved ones. Give them peace as they get through the day. As the world continues to fight through one virus after another, help us to dive deeper into Your word and depend solely on You. Help us to be fearless and not fearful, courageous and not cowardly, strong and not weak. Bless us with the ability to be the answer to someone's prayers.

Thank You for being a loving and gracious God and for forgiving us when we fall short. We love You because You first loved us. In the name of Jesus we pray, Amen.

Scripture:

"God is our refuge and strength, a very present help in trouble."

Psalm 46:1 (KJV)

Day 11
There Is Still Hope

Father God, we thank You for this day, a new day filled with new opportunities. Today is a day where we should be thankful that we not only have a chance to be a blessing to someone else, but we have a chance to be the answer to someone's prayers. As we enjoy a day of relaxation for some, work for some, overcoming illnesses for some, laying loved ones to rest, or simply a day of reflection for some, help us to know that in this life where the future is uncertain, where families are falling apart, where drugs are running rampant throughout our communities, and people are dying left and right, there is still hope.

Father, we thank You that in the midst of all the chaos, we can have peace and joy in our hearts, fulfillment in our lives, and the power and strength to live wholesome and meaningful lives. Thank You for Your mercy and Your grace. Thank You for Your peace that surpasses all understanding. Forgive us when we mistreat each other and forget who we are in You. Thank You for loving us more than we deserve. In Jesus name we pray, Amen.

Scripture:
"Now the God of hope fill you with all joy and peace in believing, that ye may abound in hope through the power of the Holy Ghost." Romans 15:13 (KJV)

Day 12
Grateful for Your Daily Strength

* * *

Father God, thank You for this first day of the week, a day that is set aside to worship You in spirit and in truth. Although it is cold and raining outside, we are grateful for a roof over our heads, food on our tables, and clothes on our backs, all of which we can sometimes take for granted. Thank You for the strength and the courage that You give us each and every day. Thank You for blessing us with the resources to be able to be the answer to someone's prayers.

Help us as we go through each day, being bold in our understanding of who we are in You. Grant us peace in a world that has gone mad and is filled with misunderstandings. Be with those who are grieving today and give them a sense of peace. Thank You for loving us more than we love ourselves. It is in Your son Jesus name we pray, Amen.

Scripture:

"This is the day which the Lord hath made; we will rejoice and be glad in it."

Psalm 118:24 (KJV)

Day 13
A New Day with New Possibilities

Thank You Father for this beautiful day. The weather outside may be cold, but the fact that we woke up this morning is a beautiful blessing. There are so many who are sick and many who are dealing with the loss of loved ones. Be with those who are grieving this morning and encircle them with Your peace, Your love, and Your understanding. Give them the support they need to get through this day.

Father God, we know that life is short and that there are no promises for tomorrow. We are grateful that You have given us a new day with new opportunities, tremendous possibilities, and the power to be a blessing to someone in need. Give us strength to be bold in our business, in our friendships, in our personal lives, and as we walk in favor of who we are in You. We love You for who You are and because You loved us first. It is in the name of Jesus we pray, Amen.

Scripture:
"This is the day that the Lord hath made; we will rejoice and be glad in it."
Psalm 118:24 (KJV)

Day 14
Strength for the Journey

———— ❧ ————

Father God, thank You for this day and for all the blessings You have bestowed upon us. Thank You for Your love and mercy and for forgiving us when we fall short in our mistreatment of others and ourselves. Thank You for providing the sunshine so that we can appreciate the rain and the joy so we can find comfort in the midst of our pain.

Guide our footsteps while we run this race that can often be difficult. Grant peace to those who are sick, suffering, and mourning the loss of loved ones. Thank You for giving us the strength to be the answer to someone's prayers. It is in the name of Jesus that we pray, Amen.

Scripture:

"Let us run with patience the race that is set before us, looking unto Jesus the author and finisher of our faith."

Hebrews 12:1–2 (KJV)

Day 15

Thankful for Closed Doors and Open Windows

Father God, thank You so much for this day and all of the marvelous wonder it holds. Thank You for every closed door that led to an open window that no man can close. Thank You for every blessing and every opportunity that we took advantage of to be the answer to someone's prayers. Give us strength as we end our day to reflect on the things we could have done but did not do, and the things we should not have done yet did anyway.

Forgive us when we fall short, and help us to be better and do better. Thank You for Your love, Your grace, and Your mercy. In the name of Jesus we pray, Amen.

Scripture:

"And we know that all things work together for good to them that love God, to them who are the called according to his purpose."

Romans 8:28 (KJV)

Day 16
Peace for the Closing of the Day

Father, we thank You for this day and for all the opportunities that came our way. We are grateful for every blessing and for the ability to be the answer to someone's prayer. As we bring our day to a close, we thank You in advance for a peaceful night's rest. Be with those who are struggling through sickness and disease, chronic pain, and mental and emotional anguish.

Comfort those who are mourning the loss of loved ones and grant them peace that passes all understanding. We thank You for Your grace and Your mercy that fail not. Continue to strengthen us as we put our faith, our trust, and our hope in You. We pray this prayer in the name of Your son Jesus Christ, Amen.

Scripture:

"I will both lay me down in peace, and sleep, for thou, Lord, only makest me dwell in safety."

Psalm 4:8 (KJV)

Day 17
Guide Our Steps, Shape Our Hearts

*Thank You Father God for this day and for
Your love and the blessings You bestow upon
us, blessings that we do not deserve. Thank
You for the desire to motivate and encourage
others. Guide our feet so that we may walk in
accordance with Your will. Guide our tongue
so that our words will be spoken in truth.
Guide our heart so that we will do all things
based on a love like Jesus. Help us to always
do what is right even when the world around
us does not agree.*

*Forgive us when we act or react in a manner
that shows we have forgotten how awesome
and mighty You are. Touch the hearts of the
people reading this message and bless them so
they will take time to be a blessing to someone*

else. Forgive us when we fall short. This we pray in the name of Jesus, Amen.

Scripture:

"Order my steps in thy word, and let not any iniquity have dominion over me."

Psalm 119:133 (KJV)

Day 18
Tired, But Still Trusting

Are you tired? I know I am. Tired of sickness and death. Tired of pain and sorrow. Tired of dashed dreams and broken promises. Tired of evil people and watching the people I love suffer through sickness. Especially tired of this pandemic. But what I am not tired of is praying. I am not tired of leaning and depending on God. I am not tired of being obedient to His word. I am not tired of love.

Father God, You never promised that all our days would be easy. We know that we are not alone in what we are going through. Every pain, every trial, and every burden we carry, You feel them too because You love us. Help us to allow these times to grow our faith. Help us to appreciate and recognize our blessings. It is in the name of Jesus that we pray, Amen.

Scripture:

"Come unto me, all ye that labor and are heavy laden, and I will give you rest."

Matthew 11:28 (KJV)

Day 19
Rest in His Loving Arms

Father God, we are so grateful for this first day of the week. Thank You for this day that has been set aside to worship You. As we prepare ourselves for rest, we ask that You be with us through the night. Bless us with sweet dreams as we sleep. Be with those who are struggling and do not know which direction to turn. Be with those who are mourning the loss of loved ones. Be with those who feel lost and cannot seem to find their way. Thank You for the comfort of Your loving arms. It is in the name of Jesus we pray, Amen.

Scripture:
"I will both lay me down in peace, and sleep, for thou, Lord, only makest me dwell in safety."
Psalm 4:8 (KJV)

Day 20
Steadfast, Unmovable, Unshakable

*Father God, thank You for this day and for all
the love and grace You have placed within it.
In the midst of our storms, help us not to focus
so much on ourselves but to find ways to be a
blessing to others while glorifying You. Help
us to be steadfast in our purpose, unmovable
in our position, and unshakable in our faith.*

*Help us to stand firm in Your word and not
allow the actions of others to cause us to lose
sight of who You are and who we are in You.
Give us the strength to see the clear picture
when our eyes become cloudy with the things
of this world. Forgive us when we fall short
and help us to love others as You love us. In
the name of Jesus we pray, Amen.*

Scripture:

"Therefore, my beloved brethren, be ye steadfast, unmovable, always abounding in the work of the Lord, forasmuch as ye know that your labor is not in vain in the Lord."
1 Corinthians 15:58 (KJV)

Day 21
Growing in Faith, Resting in Grace

Thank You Father God for this day. As some of us begin to retire for the evening and others are starting the day, we are thankful for all the opportunities that You bless us with. Help those who struggle from day to day. Grant peace to those who are mourning the loss of friends and loved ones. Help us to shrink in fear as we grow in faith. Thank You for allowing us to be the answer to someone's prayers. Grant us Your grace and Your mercy. It is in the name of Jesus that we pray, Amen.

Scripture:
"God is our refuge and strength, a very present help in trouble."
Psalm 46:1 (KJV)

Day 22
Strength to Love and Live Right

Father God, thank You for this beautiful day that is overflowing with new possibilities. Thank You for the opportunity to be the answer to someone's prayers. Give us strength to be fair when others around us are unfair and to always conduct ourselves decently and in order. Teach us to trust You as much as we say we love You and to treat everyone with real love and kindness. Open our hearts and keep our minds stayed on You. Thank You for being our strength and our shield. In the mighty name of Jesus, Amen.

Scripture:
"Trust in the Lord with all thine heart and lean not unto thine own understanding."
Proverbs 3:5 (KJV)

Day 23
Blessings Within the Storm

Father God, thank You for this day. Often we get so caught up in the storms that are raging in our lives that we forget to give thanks for the blessings within the storms. Thank You for the love and care that You so freely give us. Help us to do what we can, when we can, in a way that truly blesses others. We love You because You loved us first. Give us the strength to hold on tight to You when the storms become so fierce that we feel knocked to and fro and want to let go. Continue to bless us as we bless others. In the name of Jesus we pray, Amen.

Scripture:
"God is our refuge and strength, a very present help in trouble."
Psalm 46:1 (KJV)

Day 24

Blessed in the Midst of It All

Father God, thank You for this day, a day that was filled with wonder and abundance. Thank You for the love You give us so freely, even when we do not deserve it. As we close out this day and look forward to tomorrow, we ask that You continue to bless us in the midst of our circumstances. Be with those who are suffering, struggling, and have lost their way. Bless those who are trying to figure out how to live without their loved ones. Give us strength to truly be the answer to someone else's prayers. In the name of Jesus we pray, Amen.

Scripture:
"The Lord is nigh unto them that are of a broken heart and saveth such as be of a contrite spirit."
Psalm 34:18 (KJV)

Day 25
Strength to Love, Grace to Forgive

Father God, thank You for Your loving kindness toward Your children. Thank You for Your mercy, for without it the world would be much worse than it already is. Forgive those who cause pain and destruction while taking Your mercy for granted. Thank You for waking us up this morning with a fresh mind. Give us strength to be kind and fair to others. Forgive us when we know the right thing to do but choose something different because of our worldly positions.

Help us to give and not take, to love and not hate, and to be gentle with the fragile. We love You and we thank You for Your grace. It is in the name of Jesus that we pray, Amen.

Scripture:

"Be ye kind one to another, tenderhearted, forgiving one another, even as God for Christ's sake hath forgiven you."

Ephesians 4:32 (KJV)

Day 26
Grateful for Grace, Anchored in Victory

Father God, thank You for Your grace and mercy, for it is what keeps us from day to day. Thank You for the assurance of knowing that as long as we have faith in You and obey Your word, victory is ours. Touch this cold, dark world with a warm, shining light so we may truly understand the magnitude of Your love. Forgive us when we fall short and turn our hearts from You. Thank You for loving us more than we could ever love ourselves. This we pray in the name of Jesus, Amen.

Scripture:
"But thanks be to God, which giveth us the victory through our Lord Jesus Christ."
1 Corinthians 15:57 (KJV)

Day 27

Overflowing with Joy

Father God, when I think about how awesome You are, I am overflowed with joy. Your love for a world sinking in sin is so amazing because You continue to bestow mercy on us when we do not deserve it. Thank You Lord for loving us that much. As some of us retire for the night and others rise for the day, we thank You for Your continued blessings. Grant us strength to face the days ahead and give us peace. I pray this prayer in the name of Jesus the Son, Amen.

Scripture:
"The Lord is good to all, and his tender mercies are over all his works."
Psalm 145:9 (KJV)

Day 28
Exceedingly, Abundantly, Above All

Thank You Lord for this day and all that is within it. Thank You for doing exceedingly and abundantly more than our minds could ever imagine. When things get tough, as they often will, thank You for providing a way of escape. Thank You for sending Your son Jesus as our Savior.

Thank You for being a comfort when our loved ones leave us, when our friends forsake us, when the roads get rough, and when the hills feel too hard to climb. Thank You for blessing us enough so that we have more than enough to be the answer to someone's prayers. We love You because You first loved us. In the name of Jesus we pray, Amen.

Scripture:

"Now unto him that is able to do exceeding abundantly above all that we ask or think, according to the power that worketh in us."

Ephesians 3:20 (KJV)

Day 29
Courage in the Midst of Fear

―――― ◯ ☀ ◯ ――――

Father God, thank You so much for this day. Thank You for giving us courage in the midst of fear. Thank You for helping us to be strong even when we feel like falling apart. Help us to put our trust and our faith in You. Help us to depend on You and not the world. Forgive us when we fall short of Your will and Your way. Thank You for loving us more than we deserve. In the name of Jesus we pray, Amen.

Scripture:
"Fear thou not, for I am with thee. Be not dismayed, for I am thy God. I will strengthen thee, yea, I will help thee, yea, I will uphold thee with the right hand of my righteousness."
Isaiah 41:10 (KJV)

Day 30
Strength for the Climb

Father God, thank You for giving us the strength to climb our mountains and for leading us around our stumbling blocks. You are Lord of creation, and we are grateful to You for loving us with an unconditional love. Thank You for blessing us so we can be a blessing to others. Forgive us when we fall short. In the name of Your son Jesus we pray, Amen.

Scripture:
"The Lord is my strength and my shield. My heart trusted in him, and I am helped."
Psalm 28:7 (KJV)

Day 31
Guarding Our Thoughts

Father God, remove negativity from our paths. Let us not allow other people's negative thoughts to become our negative thoughts, and do not let our negative thoughts become someone else's negative thoughts. If a negative thought should enter our minds, I ask that You kill it before it exits our mouth. Grant us Your love, Your grace, and Your mercy. In Jesus name we pray, Amen.

Scripture:
"Let the words of my mouth, and the meditation of my heart, be acceptable in thy sight, O Lord, my strength and my redeemer."
Psalm 19:14 (KJV)

Day 32
Looking Ahead with Wisdom and Grace

Thank You Father God for this day and all the opportunities and possibilities that it holds. Thank You for Your loving grace that You continue to bestow on my life. Lord, give me wisdom in mind, strength in body, and purity in heart to do Your will. Help me to look ahead, and only look behind as a reminder of where I am going and not where I still am. Help me to be a shining light and a motivating factor in the lives of others. Forgive me when I fall short. In the name of Jesus, Amen.

Scripture:
"If any of you lack wisdom, let him ask of God, that giveth to all men liberally, and upbraideth not, and it shall be given him."
James 1:5 (KJV)

Day 33
Blessings Upon Blessings

Father God, thank You for this day. Thank You for the blessings upon blessings upon blessings that You have bestowed upon us on this day. Forgive us when we take Your blessings for granted. Forgive us when we do not appreciate the things we have and still want more. Forgive us when we fail to consider those who are less fortunate than we are.

Thank You for helping us to be a blessing to those who are in need. Thank You for blessing us with enough so that we can be the answer to someone else's prayers. Thank You for loving us more than we deserve. Keep us safe and give us peace. In Jesus name we pray, Amen.

Scripture:

"O give thanks unto the Lord, for he is good,
for his mercy endureth forever."
Psalm 107:1 (KJV)

Day 34
Walking by Faith

Father God, thank You for the ability to love when we are hurt, to laugh when we want to cry, and to smile when we are sad. Help us to always trust You, even when the days are dark and stormy. Grant us Your grace and Your mercy. Help us to walk by faith and not by sight. We thank You and we love You. In Jesus name we pray, Amen.

Scripture:
"For we walk by faith, not by sight."
2 Corinthians 5:7 (KJV)

Day 35
With You, We Are Everything

Thank You Father God for the beauty of this day. With You we are everything, but without You we are nothing. Help us to continue to let our lights shine. In Jesus name we pray, Amen.

Scripture:
"Let your light so shine before men, that they may see your good works, and glorify your Father which is in heaven."
Matthew 5:16 (KJV)

Day 36
Peace in the Midst of the Storm

Father God, thank You for the blessings of this day. Thank You for Your unmerited favor, which we do not deserve. Be with those who are sinking in the depths of despair because of sickness, sadness, and grief. Give us peace in the midst of our storms. Thank You for Your love and grace. Forgive us when we fall short and forget that we each have the capacity to help someone in need and be the answer to their prayers. In the name of Jesus we pray, Amen.

Scripture:
"Peace I leave with you, my peace I give unto you. Not as the world giveth, give I unto you. Let not your heart be troubled, neither let it be afraid."
John 14:27 (KJV)

Day 37
Peace in the Midst of Chaos

Thank You Lord for this day and for helping us be content in the midst of chaos. When life seems to be spinning out of control, You are the peace. We love You because You loved us first. In the name of Jesus we pray, Amen.

Scripture:
"Thou wilt keep him in perfect peace, whose mind is stayed on thee, because he trusteth in thee."
Isaiah 26:3 (KJV)

Day 38
Loving Beyond the Pain

———— ❦ ————

Father God, we thank You for this day. Thank You for the ability to love past pain. We know that hurt and pain are real, feelings of depression and despair are real, grief and heartache are real, but so are You. Thank You for being a constant in the midst of chaos. Yesterday I had to remind myself that everyone has an agenda, including me.

Everyone has a reason, good or bad, right or wrong, for why they do what they do. Some people have the mindset to do whatever it takes to get what they want, regardless of how much pain they cause or who they hurt. But I am grateful that as Christians we are called to do better, to be the light, and to let Your peace rule in us. Help us to be mindful of how we treat people. Forgive us when we pass up opportunities to be a blessing to others. In the name of Jesus we pray, Amen.

Scripture:
"And let the peace of God rule in your hearts, to the which also ye are called in one body, and be ye thankful."
Colossians 3:15 (KJV)

Day 39
Grateful for the Simple Blessings

———— ⊙ ✹ ⊙ ————

Thank You Father God for all the wonderful blessings You have bestowed upon us this day. Thank You for the material blessings that we often take for granted—for warm beds, roofs over our heads, and food on our tables, thank You. Help us to be mindful of those who are less fortunate and wish they had even a morsel of what we have. Give us the ability to love others as You love us. Forgive us when we fall short. In the name of Jesus we pray, Amen.

Scripture:
"In every thing give thanks, for this is the will of God in Christ Jesus concerning you."
1 Thessalonians 5:18 (KJV)

Day 40
Content in Every Circumstance

Father God, thank You for helping me learn to appreciate my blessings. I am a living witness that it is possible to be content in the midst of chaos. When life seems to be spinning out of control, thank You for helping me find a way to live peacefully. Knowing that You are my source of strength and that You love me and care for me gives me peace. Therefore, I am content, and I have learned to be content whatever the circumstances. Thank You for Your grace and mercy. Forgive me when I fall short. In the name of Jesus I pray, Amen.

Scripture:
"Not that I speak in respect of want, for I have learned, in whatsoever state I am, therewith to be content."
Philippians 4:11 (KJV)

Day 41
A Circle of Never-Ending Love

Let's talk about love.

If love was a rainbow, it would be a circle.

Traveling around the circle would be the Fruit of the Spirit (Galatians 5:22–23). In the center there would be a crystal pot filled with the characteristics of the Godhead, worth more than gold.

In the pot would be patience, kindness, rejoicing in truth, forbearance, hope, endurance, and a heart that is not suspicious. The rainbow would be a unified consistency of love that never ends, because Love Never Fails (1 Corinthians 13:8).

Father God, thank You for this day, this day of love. Thank You for being more than words, candy, or flowers spoken on a certain day. Thank You for helping us realize that true love lives in the hearts of those who love like Jesus. In His name we pray, Amen.

Scripture:

"Beloved, let us love one another, for love is of God, and everyone that loveth is born of God and knoweth God."

1 John 4:7 (KJV)

Day 42
Thank You for Every Answer

Father God, thank You for answered prayers. Thank You for the yes, thank You for the no, and thank You for the just wait. Grant us wisdom from day to day. In the name of Jesus we pray, Amen.

Scripture:
"If any of you lack wisdom, let him ask of God, that giveth to all men liberally, and upbraideth not, and it shall be given him."
James 1:5 (KJV)

Day 43
Kindness in an Unkind World

Thank You Father for this day and the wonderful blessings contained within it. Help us to be kind, even when others are unkind to us. Help us as we put our faith and confidence in You and not in the world. Give us the strength to love those who behave in unlovable ways. Help us to recognize when we have the ability to be the answer to someone's prayers. Forgive us when we fall short. In the name of Jesus we pray, Amen.

Scripture:
"Be not overcome of evil, but overcome evil with good."
Romans 12:21 (KJV)

Day 44
God, You Are Truly Amazing

Thank You God for being truly amazing. You continuously look out for us. We thank You for blessing us so that we can be a blessing to others. We give You all glory, honor, and praise. In Jesus name we pray, Amen.

Scripture:
"O give thanks unto the Lord, for he is good, for his mercy endureth forever."
Psalm 107:1 (KJV)

Day 45
Decreasing Self, Increasing You

———— ❦ ————

Thank You Father God for the magnitude of love You have shown to the world from the very beginning. Thank You for bestowing Your grace and mercy on us over and over again. Help us to be good stewards and to walk in the light of Your love by obeying Your holy word. Help us as we decrease in self and increase in You. Forgive us for not loving enough and not being obedient enough. Forgive us when we fall short of Your word and lose focus of our purpose. Bless us and keep us all safe. In the name of Jesus we pray, Amen.

Scripture:
"He must increase, but I must decrease."
John 3:30 (KJV)

Day 46
Sometimes Thank You Is Enough

Father God, sometimes all we need to do is say thank You. Amen.

Scripture:
"In every thing give thanks, for this is the will of God in Christ Jesus concerning you."
1 Thessalonians 5:18 (KJV)

Day 47
Thank You for the Rain

Father God, thank You for the rain that washes the earth. Thank You for the rain in our lives that helps us grow closer and stronger in Your word. As we journey through this day, help us to be a blessing to someone else. In the name of Jesus we pray, Amen.

Scripture:
"He shall come down like rain upon the mown grass, as showers that water the earth."
Psalm 72:6 (KJV)

Day 48
A "Son" Shining Day

Thank You Father for this beautiful Son shining day. Thank You for loving us enough to show us an example of true love and sacrifice. Help us as we shine our lights, and give us strength to be the answer to someone's prayers. In the name of Jesus we pray, Amen.

Scripture:
"For God so loved the world, that he gave his only begotten Son."
John 3:16 (KJV)

Day 49
Strength for the Journey

Thank You Father God for this day. Thank You for helping our light to shine so we may be a blessing to those in need. Strengthen us on this journey where we are weak. Help us to stay on task and not lose focus of our eternal purpose. Thank You for loving us so much that You sent Your son Jesus into the world to die a painful death to save a world lost in sin.

Forgive us when we fall short and restore us to a right position. We thank You for the many blessings You have bestowed upon our lives. Touch the hearts and minds of our family and friends who read this prayer that they may be blessed. This we pray in the matchless name of Jesus, the One who saves, Amen.

Scripture:

"The Lord is my light and my salvation; whom shall I fear?"

Psalm 27:1 (KJV)

Day 50
Kept by His Grace

———— ❋ ————

Thank You Father God for keeping us in the midst of it all. Father God, our hearts and our minds are open to You. We love You because of who You are, for loving us, and for never leaving us. Your grace is sufficient. In Jesus name we pray, Amen.

Scripture:
"My grace is sufficient for thee, for my strength is made perfect in weakness."
2 Corinthians 12:9 (KJV)

Day 51
Thankful in All Things

Thank You God for this day. In all things we give You thanks. For waking us up this morning, for the food on our tables, and for the roofs over our heads, we say thank You. For wisdom to seek Your direction and not be swayed by the troubles of the world, we say thank You. In the mighty name of Jesus we pray, Amen.

Scripture:
"In every thing give thanks, for this is the will of God in Christ Jesus concerning you."
1 Thessalonians 5:18 (KJV)

Day 52
Growing Stronger in You

Father God, thank You for this day and all that it possesses— the good, the bad, and the ugly. We are grateful for every test and every opportunity to grow stronger in Your word and in our eternal purpose. Give us strength as we grow. Help us to increase in You as we decrease in ourselves. In the name of Jesus we pray, Amen.

Scripture:
"He must increase, but I must decrease."
John 3:30 (KJV)

Day 53
A Willing Heart and an Uncompromised Walk

Father God, thank You for this beautiful day. I pray for an open heart directed by Your word, a heart willing to walk in the light of that word. Father, if anything stands in the path of Your word, give me the resolve and honesty to remove it from my life, even if it is family, friends, fellow saints, or foes. Help me to recognize the relevance of Your word in my life today and in this present moment.

I thank You for the flawless and sinless model You gave us, Your Son Jesus. I am mindful of Him leaving a perfect heaven of light and holiness to come to this dark world where His own rejected Him. They spit in His face, beat Him, denied Him, hated Him, and drove spikes into His hands and feet, and with His love He said, "Father, forgive them." May the model of Jesus strengthen me to make changes so that I continue moving in the right direction and break the habits that lead me in the wrong direction. Use Your word to radically shape my thinking toward Your will instead of my own. Thank You God for loving me in spite of me. In Your Son Jesus name, Amen.

Scripture:
"Thy word is a lamp unto my feet, and a light unto my path."
Psalm 119:105 (KJV)

Day 54
Sustained by Grace

Thank You Lord for Your daily grace and Your mercy that sustains me. The air that fills my lungs is a blessing from You, giving me another opportunity to spread Your love. You alone are worthy of my praise. Thank You for the sacrifice of Your Son Jesus, and it is in His name I pray, Amen.

Scripture:
"Let every thing that hath breath praise the Lord."
Psalm 150:6 (KJV)

Day 55
Grateful for Every Open Door

Thank You Father God for a day filled with peace and love. We are grateful for every open door that leads us closer to You. Forgive us when we fall short and fail to be a blessing to others. Thank You for loving us before we even knew ourselves. In the name of Jesus we pray, Amen.

Scripture:
"We love him, because he first loved us."
1 John 4:19 (KJV)

Day 56
A Heart That Loves Like You

─── ❋ ───

Heavenly Father, thank You for waking me up this morning and showing me grace and mercy through Your love. Thank You for showing me how to love from the heart, even loving those who mean harm to my life. Thank You for giving me an open mind and a willing heart to understand the truth of Your plan of salvation. Help me to be a shining light in a world of darkness.

Bless my family and friends as they go about their day. Forgive me for my sins and help me to be a blessing to someone else. In the righteous name of Jesus I pray, Amen.

Scripture:

"Let your light so shine before men, that they may see your good works, and glorify your Father which is in heaven."

Matthew 5:16 (KJV)

Day 57
Bold Faith, Shining Light

Father God, thank You for waking me up this morning and for Your infinite wisdom. Thank You for sending Your Son Jesus as the light to a world living in darkness. Thank You for being in my heart and for every opportunity to touch the lives of others. Help me to stand strong and be bold in my faith and in my beliefs. Help me to let my God-light shine for those struggling to find their way out of darkness. Touch the lives of the people reading this prayer so that they may be blessed. Be in my heart continually and help me to be a blessing to someone else. Forgive me when I repent of my sins and restore me to a right position in You. Thank You for loving me more than I deserve and for never leaving or

forsaking me. This I pray in Your Son Jesus name, Amen.

Scripture:

"The Lord is my light and my salvation; whom shall I fear?"

Psalm 27:1 (KJV)

Day 58
Strengthen Me Where I Am Weak

Father God, I just want to say thank You. Thank You for loving us more than anyone or anything on this earth could ever possess the capability to. Thank You for Your mercy and Your continued grace. Help me to be the faithful woman You are calling me to be. Thank You for every opportunity to grow stronger in Your word so that I can share the good news of Your love and Your plan of eternal salvation. Strengthen me where I am weak. Forgive me when I sin and fall short of Your glory. Help me to walk my talk daily so that I can be a blessing to someone else. This I pray in the mighty name of Jesus, Amen.

Scripture:

"My flesh and my heart faileth, but God is the strength of my heart and my portion forever."
Psalm 73:26 (KJV)

Day 59
Let My Words Reflect Your Love

Thank You Father God for health and strength. Thank You for being a loving God and a forgiving God. As I journey throughout this day, help me to be a blessing to those I come in contact with. Let the words that flow from my lips reflect the love that flows from my heart. Forgive me when I fall short and restore me to a right position in You. This I pray in Your son Jesus name, Amen.

Scripture:
"Let your speech be always with grace, seasoned with salt."
Colossians 4:6 (KJV)

Day 60
Trust God in Every Season

Sometimes in your darkest hours, the light shines the brightest. In the midst of your storms, in the center of your despair... trust God. When the billows are raging and the struggles of life seem too heavy to bear... trust God. When you are trying to get up but keep falling down... trust God. When days are so difficult that all you want to do is cry—trust me, I've been there—put your faith in God, pray, and trust Him. Remember, obedience to God has its own benefits. Father God, help me to trust and depend on You more. In the name of Jesus I pray, Amen.

Scripture:
"Trust in the Lord with all thine heart, and lean not unto thine own understanding."
Proverbs 3:5 (KJV)

Day 61
A Guiding Light in the World

Thank You Father God for this day. As I prepare to leave my home and go out into the world, help me to be a blessing to the people I come in contact with. Help me to find the positive in every situation. Help me to be the guiding light to those trying to find their way out of darkness. Let the truth in my heart radiate through my words and actions.

Forgive me when I forget the awesome power of Your love and place limitations on You. Forgive me when I fall short and restore me to a right position in You. Help me to remember and embrace the importance of family. Bless the people reading this prayer so they may be blessed and be a blessing to someone else. This I pray in the mighty, matchless name of Jesus, Amen.

Scripture:

"Thy word is a lamp unto my feet, and a light unto my path."

Psalm 119:105 (KJV)

Day 62
A Day Lived in Purpose

Father God, as I prepare to bring my day to an end, I thank You for waking me up this morning with purpose in my heart to do Your blessed will. As I continue this amazing faith walk, help me to do those things that are right and pleasing to You. Help me to be a guiding light to those seeking a way out of darkness. Forgive me when I fall short and bless me abundantly in my sincere efforts. Thank You for every open door and every opportunity to share the truth of Your love. In Jesus name I pray, Amen.

Scripture:
"Commit thy works unto the Lord, and thy thoughts shall be established."
Proverbs 16:3 (KJV)

Day 63
Strength to Endure

Lord, I thank You for this day. Thank You for Your grace and mercy as I made it through this first day of the week. Forgive me for anything I have said or done that did not represent the Christian woman I strive to be. Give me strength to endure and to persevere in spite of all I see around me. In the mighty name of Jesus I pray, Amen.

Scripture:
"But they that wait upon the Lord shall renew their strength."
Isaiah 40:31 (KJV)

Day 64
Staying Grounded in His Word

Father God, I am so grateful for all the blessings of this day. Thank You for Your tremendous love and care for me. Be with those who are struggling to find their way to You. Help me stay grounded and focused in Your word. In the name of Jesus I pray, Amen.

Scripture:
"Draw nigh to God, and he will draw nigh to you."
James 4:8 (KJV)

Day 65
To God Be the Glory

To God be the glory for the things He has done. In the mighty name of Jesus, Amen.

Scripture:
"Not unto us, O Lord, not unto us, but unto thy name give glory."
Psalm 115:1 (KJV)

Day 66
A Way Out of No Way

Father God, thank You for being a way out of no way. Thank You for the open window when the door has been nailed shut. Thank You for Your grace and Your mercy. Thank You for Your love. In the name of Jesus I pray, Amen.

Scripture:
"Behold, I am the Lord, the God of all flesh. Is there anything too hard for me?"
Jeremiah 32:27 (KJV)

Day 67
Guide My Steps in Your Light

Thank You Father for Your grace and mercy, for without it we would be lost with no direction. Thank You for peace of mind and for the ability to see the me that man cannot see. Help me grow stronger and wiser in Your word. Direct my footsteps as I walk in the light of Your love. In the matchless name of Jesus I pray, Amen.

Scripture:
"The steps of a good man are ordered by the Lord."
Psalm 37:23 (KJV)

Day 68
A Prayer of Encouragement

Father God, thank You for this beautiful day. I pray for an open heart directed by Your word that leads to a willingness to walk in the light of that word. Father, if anything stands in the path of Your word, give me the resolve and honesty to remove it from my life, even if it is family, friends, fellow saints, or foes. Help me to recognize the relevance of Your word in my life today and in this present moment.

I thank You for the flawless and sinless model You gave us, Your Son Jesus. I am mindful of Him leaving a perfect heaven of light and holiness to come to a dark world where His own rejected Him. They spit in His face, beat Him, denied Him, hated Him, and drove spikes into His hands and feet, and with His love He said, "Father, forgive them." May the model of Jesus strengthen me to make changes so I can continue moving in the right direction and break habits that lead me in the wrong direction. Use Your word to radically alter my thinking toward Your will instead of my own. Thank You God for loving me in spite of me. In Your Son Jesus name, Amen.

Scripture:
"Create in me a clean heart, O God, and renew a right spirit within me."
Psalm 51:10 (KJV)

Day 69
Praise Through the Storm

How you go through your storm determines how you come out of your storm. If you go through the storm depressed, beaten, and broken, then when your storm is over you will not recognize it. Praise God continually through your storm.

Thank You Lord for waking me up this morning and giving me the opportunity to praise Your holy name in the midst of my storm. Thank You for Your grace and mercy. Thank You for surrounding me with people of like faith. Forgive me for my sins and thank You for restoring me when I fall short. Let me be a shining example to help others know how to praise You while they are going through their storms. This prayer I ask in the matchless name of Jesus, Amen.

Scripture:

"I will bless the Lord at all times. His praise shall continually be in my mouth."

Psalm 34:1 (KJV)

Day 70
Attitude Check

No matter what happens in our lives, our attitude and how we view the situation make all the difference in the world. Looking for different outcomes? Try doing an attitude check.

Thank You Lord for this day and all that it holds. Help me keep the right attitude, the right frame of mind, and the right heart. Forgive me when I lose myself and become entangled with the thoughts and feelings of the world. It is in the precious name of Jesus I pray, Amen.

Scripture:
"Let this mind be in you, which was also in Christ Jesus."
Philippians 2:5 (KJV)

Day 71

Prayer Does Not Fix Disobedience

Prayer does not fix disobedience. Every day that we live is an opportunity to choose to do right or do wrong, to grow and draw closer to God or to pull away from Him. We must live our lives on purpose and with purpose. Oftentimes we want to pray for God to fix our shortcomings and our sinful actions, and while the Word teaches us to pray without ceasing, we must also choose to obey.

As Christians, following Christ is the best decision one can make for eternal salvation. "See then that ye walk circumspectly, not as fools, but as wise, redeeming the time because the days are evil. Wherefore be ye not unwise, but understanding what the will of the Lord is."
Ephesians 5:15–17 (KJV)

Friends, the world would have us believe that we can do whatever we want and say whatever we want without consequences, but beware—our eternal end will be justified by our earthly living. Just a little something to ponder... some food for thought.

Loving you out loud, on purpose, with purpose. Be blessed in your day.

Day 72
Soul-Beautifying Choices

Father God, in the midst of my decision-making, give me the strength to look to You for guidance and not man. Help my choices to be soul beautifying and not sinful or selfish. Grant me courage to change the person I see in the mirror of truth I hold before me. Give me a heart of pure love that withstands the bitter darkness. Keep me on the path that is light directed and covered in Your mercy. Forgive me when I fall short and miss the mark. Today and every day, thank You for Your undying love for me. This is my prayer in Your Son Jesus name, Amen.

Friends, I love you and there is nothing— absolutely nothing—you can do about it.

Scripture:

"Create in me a clean heart, O God, and renew a right spirit within me."

Psalm 51:10 (KJV)

Day 73
Look to the Hills

Lord, I thank You for this day and all that is within it.

God is able to do exceedingly and abundantly more than our minds could ever imagine. When things get tough—as they often will— rest assured that God has already provided a way of escape. He sent His only Son Jesus to take away the sins of the world.

So when you think you have taken all you can take, look to the hills. When your burdens seem too heavy to bear, look to the hills. When friends forsake you and enemies come for you, look to the hills, for your help is already there, waiting for you to reach out.

Take time to be a blessing to someone else today; the power to do so lies within you.

Have an awesome day. Loving you on purpose with purpose.

Scripture:

"I will lift up mine eyes unto the hills, from whence cometh my help. My help cometh from the Lord."

Psalm 121:1–2 (KJV)

Day 74
Encourage Yourself in the Lord

Thank You Lord for this day. Thank You for those who help strengthen my being. Help me to be that shining light You are calling me to be. Forgive me when I allow my physical condition to affect my spiritual condition. When I fall short, forgive me, restore me, and be with me in my dark hours. Help me to appreciate the rainbow after the storms. When I feel alone and cannot find anyone to encourage me, give me the strength to look in the mirror and encourage myself. I pray this prayer in the mighty name of Jesus, Amen.

Scripture:
"David encouraged himself in the Lord his God."
1 Samuel 30:6 (KJV)

Day 75
Praying With the Right Heart

How many times have we cried out to God in despair, feeling as if He was not listening? How many times have we prayed for God to intervene and thought He was silent?

God is a God of love, and He cares about every detail of our lives. But if we harbor sin, refuse to give up what we know is wrong, or refuse to forgive others, we cannot expect Him to hear us. We must pray without ceasing, but with a right heart and a right spirit.

"In everything by prayer and supplication with thanksgiving let your requests be made known unto God."
Philippians 4:6 (KJV)

We must not allow trials and tribulations to discourage us from praying. When we are in a right position in Christ, we have assurance that He hears us—yet His answers come according to His will, not ours.

Friends, may we have faith strong enough to trust God whether His answer is yes, no, or wait.

Have an awesome day. Loving you out loud, on purpose, with purpose.

Closing Reflections

Thank you friends for joining me on this 75-day journey of prayer, reflection, healing, and spiritual growth. My prayer is that somewhere within these pages, you found comfort for your pain, strength for your struggles, peace for your heart, and a renewed desire to walk boldly in your God-given purpose. Prayer is not just what we do, prayer is who we are when we choose to trust God with every part of our lives.

As you move forward beyond Day 75, remember that God is still listening, still working, and still moving in ways seen and unseen. Keep praying, keep believing, and keep trusting that He is guiding your steps with love and intention.

If you have a personal prayer request or need spiritual encouragement, I would be honored to stand in prayer with you. You can reach me directly by email at:

laquita@afailure2communicate.com

If you would like to continue your journey of healing and purpose, I invite you to explore my other book titles, including:

• By God's Design, Walking in Purpose Not Permission
• And many more life-changing titles available through Pa-Pro-Vi Publishing

As an International Bestselling author, it is my joy and divine assignment to help others grow, heal, write, and walk in their purpose. If you would like to purchase any of my books or learn more about my work, please feel free to contact me. Your support means more than you know.

Thank you for allowing me to pray with you, pour into you, and walk alongside you during these 75 days. May God bless you abundantly, strengthen you continually, and surround you with His everlasting love.

Loving you out loud, on purpose, with purpose.

Dr. LaQuita Parks

CEO & Founder

Pa-Pro-Vi Publishing

www.paprovipublishing.com

www.ingramcontent.com/pod-product-compliance
Lightning Source LLC
Chambersburg PA
CBHW060404090426
42734CB00011B/2258

9 7 8 1 9 5 9 6 6 7 8 7 2